from

CW00550754

FRANCIS FRITH'S

FROME PHOTOGRAPHIC
MEMORIES

THE FRANCIS FRITH COLLECTION

www.francisfrith.com

Photographic Memories

Francis Frith's
Frome

Hilary Green

First published in the United Kingdom in 2001 by
The Francis Frith Collection

Paperback Edition 2001
ISBN 1-85937-317-8

British Library Cataloguing in Publication Data

Francis Frith's Around Frome
Hilary Green

The Francis Frith Collection
Frith's Barn, Teffont,
Salisbury, Wiltshire SP3 5QP
Tel: +44 (0) 1722 716 376
Email: info@francisfrith.co.uk
www.francisfrith.com

Printed and bound in Great Britain

Front Cover: Frome, The Oldest House 1907 58851p

The colour-tinting is for illustrative purposes only, and is not intended to be historically accurate

Contents

Francis Frith: Victorian Pioneer 7

Frith's Archive - A Unique Legacy 10

Frome - An Introduction 12

Frome to Orchardleigh 16

Rode to Longleat 37

Back to Frome 46

Mells to Nunney 72

Index 87

Free Mounted Print Voucher 91

Francis Frith: *Victorian Pioneer*

FRANCIS FRITH, Victorian founder of the world-famous photographic archive, was a complex and multi-talented man. A devout Quaker and a highly successful Victorian businessman, he was both philosophic by nature and pioneering in outlook.

By 1855 Francis Frith had already established a wholesale grocery business in Liverpool, and sold it for the astonishing sum of £200,000, which is the equivalent today of over £15,000,000. Now a multi-millionaire, he was able to indulge his passion for travel. As a child he had pored over travel books written by early explorers, and his fancy and imagination had been stirred by family holidays to the sublime mountain regions of Wales and Scotland. 'What a land of spirit-stirring and enriching scenes and places!' he had written. He was to return to these scenes of grandeur in later years to 'recapture the thousands of vivid and tender memories', but with a different purpose. Now in his thirties, and captivated by the new science of photography, Frith set out on a series of pioneering journeys to the Nile regions that occupied him from 1856 until 1860.

Intrigue and Adventure

He took with him on his travels a specially-designed wicker carriage that acted as both dark-room and sleeping chamber. These far-flung journeys were packed with intrigue and adventure. In his life story, written when he was sixty-three, Frith tells of being held captive by bandits, and of fighting 'an awful midnight battle to the very point of surrender with a deadly pack of hungry, wild dogs'. Sporting flowing Arab costume, Frith arrived at Akaba by camel seventy years before Lawrence, where he encountered 'desert princes and rival sheikhs, blazing with jewel-hilted swords'.

During these extraordinary adventures he was assiduously exploring the desert regions bordering the Nile and patiently recording the antiquities and peoples with his camera. He was the first photographer to venture beyond the sixth cataract. Africa was still the mysterious 'Dark Continent', and Stanley and Livingstone's historic meeting was a decade into the future. The conditions for picture taking confound belief. He laboured for hours in his wicker dark-room in the sweltering heat of the desert, while the volatile chemicals fizzed dangerously in their trays. Often he was forced to work in remote tombs and caves where conditions were cooler. Back in London he exhibited his photographs and was 'rapturously cheered' by members of the Royal Society. His reputation as

a photographer was made overnight. An eminent modern historian has likened their impact on the population of the time to that on our own generation of the first photographs taken on the surface of the moon.

Venture of a Life-Time

Characteristically, Frith quickly spotted the opportunity to create a new business as a specialist publisher of photographs. He lived in an era of immense and sometimes violent change. For the poor in the early part of Victoria's reign work was a drudge and the hours long, and people had precious little free time to enjoy themselves. Most had no transport other than a cart or gig at their disposal, and had not travelled far beyond the boundaries of their own town or village. However,

by the 1870s, the railways had threaded their way across the country, and Bank Holidays and half-day Saturdays had been made obligatory by Act of Parliament. All of a sudden the ordinary working man and his family were able to enjoy days out and see a little more of the world.

With characteristic business acumen, Francis Frith foresaw that these new tourists would enjoy having souvenirs to commemorate their days out. In 1860 he married Mary Ann Rosling and set out with the intention of photographing every city, town and village in Britain. For the next thirty years he travelled the country by train and by pony and trap, producing fine photographs of seaside resorts and beauty spots that were keenly bought by millions of Victorians. These prints were painstakingly pasted into family albums and pored over during the dark nights of winter, rekindling precious memories of summer excursions.

The Rise of Frith & Co

Frith's studio was soon supplying retail shops all over the country. To meet the demand he gathered about him a small team of photographers, and published the work of independent artist-photographers of the calibre of Roger Fenton and Francis Bedford. In order to gain some understanding of the scale of Frith's business one only has to look at the catalogue issued by Frith & Co in 1886: it runs to some 670 pages, listing not only many thousands of views of the British Isles but also many photographs of most European countries, and China, Japan, the USA and Canada – note the sample page shown above from the hand-written *Frith & Co* ledgers detailing pictures taken. By 1890 Frith had created the greatest specialist photographic publishing company in the

Frith's death, a new card measuring 5.5 x 3.5 inches became the standard format, but it was not until 1902 that the divided back came into being, with address and message on one face and a full-size illustration on the other. *Frith & Co* were in the vanguard of postcard development, and Frith's sons Eustace and Cyril continued their father's monumental task, expanding the number of views offered to the public and recording more and more places in Britain, as the coasts and countryside were opened up to mass travel.

Francis Frith died in 1898 at his villa in Cannes, his great project still growing. The archive he created continued in business for another seventy years. By 1970 it contained over a third of a million pictures of 7,000 cities, towns and villages. The massive photographic record Frith has left to us stands as a living monument to a special and very remarkable man.

world, with over 2,000 outlets – more than the combined number that Boots and W H Smith have today! The picture on the right shows the *Frith & Co* display board at Ingleton in the Yorkshire Dales. Beautifully constructed with mahogany frame and gilt inserts, it could display up to a dozen local scenes.

Postcard Bonanza

The ever-popular holiday postcard we know today took many years to develop. In 1870 the Post Office issued the first plain cards, with a pre-printed stamp on one face. In 1894 they allowed other publishers' cards to be sent through the mail with an attached adhesive halfpenny stamp. Demand grew rapidly, and in 1895 a new size of postcard was permitted called the court card, but there was little room for illustration. In 1899, a year after

Frith's Archive: *A Unique Legacy*

FRANCIS FRITH'S legacy to us today is of immense significance and value, for the magnificent archive of evocative photographs he created provides a unique record of change in 7,000 cities, towns and villages throughout Britain over a century and more. Frith and his fellow studio photographers revisited locations many times down the years to update their views, compiling for us an enthralling and colourful pageant of British life and character.

We tend to think of Frith's sepia views of Britain as nostalgic, for most of us use them to conjure up memories of places in our own lives with which we have family associations. It often makes us forget that to Francis Frith they were records of daily life as it was actually being lived in the cities, towns and villages of his day. The Victorian age was one of great and often bewildering change for ordinary people, and though the pictures evoke an impression of slower times, life was as busy and hectic as it is today.

We are fortunate that Frith was a photographer of the people, dedicated to recording the minutiae of everyday life. For it is this sheer wealth of visual data, the painstaking chronicle of changes in dress, transport, street layouts, buildings, housing, engineering and landscape that captivates us so much today. His remarkable images offer us a powerful link with the past and with the lives of our ancestors.

Today's Technology

Computers have now made it possible for Frith's many thousands of images to be accessed almost instantly. In the Frith archive today, each photograph is carefully 'digitised' then stored on a CD Rom. Frith archivists can locate a single photograph amongst thousands within seconds. Views can be catalogued and sorted under a variety of categories of place and content to the immediate benefit of researchers.

Inexpensive reference prints can be created for them at the touch of a mouse button, and a wide range of books and other printed materials assembled and published for a wider, more general readership - in the next twelve months over a hundred Frith local history titles will be published! The day-to-day workings of the archive are very different from how they were in Francis Frith's time: imagine the herculean task of sorting through eleven tons of glass negatives as Frith had to do to locate a particular sequence of pictures! Yet the

See Frith at www.francisfrith.com

archive still prides itself on maintaining the same high standards of excellence laid down by Francis Frith, including the painstaking cataloguing and indexing of every view.

It is curious to reflect on how the internet now allows researchers in America and elsewhere greater instant access to the archive than Frith himself ever enjoyed. Many thousands of individual views can be called up on screen within seconds on one of the Frith internet sites, enabling people living continents away to revisit the streets of their ancestral home town, or view places in Britain where they have enjoyed holidays. Many overseas researchers welcome the chance to view special theme selections, such as transport, sports, costume and ancient monuments.

We are certain that Francis Frith would have heartily approved of these modern developments in imaging techniques, for he himself was always working at the very limits of Victorian photographic technology.

The Value of the Archive Today

Because of the benefits brought by the computer, Frith's images are increasingly studied by social historians, by researchers into genealogy and ancestory, by architects, town planners, and by teachers and schoolchildren involved in local history projects.

In addition, the archive offers every one of us an opportunity to examine the places where we and our families have lived and worked down the years. Highly successful in Frith's own era, the archive is now, a century and more on, entering a new phase of popularity.

The Past in Tune with the Future

Historians consider the Francis Frith Collection to be of prime national importance. It is the only archive of its kind remaining in private ownership and has been valued at a million pounds. However, this figure is now rapidly increasing as digital technology enables more and more people around the world to enjoy its benefits.

Francis Frith's archive is now housed in an historic timber barn in the beautiful village of Teffont in Wiltshire. Its founder would not recognize the archive office as it is today. In place of the many thousands of dusty boxes containing glass plate negatives and an all-pervading odour of photographic chemicals, there are now ranks of computer screens. He would be amazed to watch his images travelling round the world at unimaginable speeds through network and internet lines.

The archive's future is both bright and exciting. Francis Frith, with his unshakeable belief in making photographs available to the greatest number of people, would undoubtedly approve of what is being done today with his lifetime's work. His photographs, depicting our shared past, are now bringing pleasure and enlightenment to millions around the world a century and more after his death.

Frome - *An Introduction*

FROME, OR FROOME, as it was originally spelt and is still pronounced, derived from the Welsh 'ffraw' meaning fair or fine, takes its name from the river which meanders along its way to join the Avon near Bath. Fair is an apt description of this market town: it rests mostly on Forest Marble, a stone much used in many of its buildings. Originally, this area was covered with forest which stretched from the English Channel to the Cotswolds, affording shelter to sparse settlements. When the Saxons finally penetrated what is known as Selwood Forest, they brought Christianity with them. St Aldhelm, Abbot of Malmesbury, who later became Bishop of Sherborne, founded a monastery here in 690, dedicating the small church to St John the Baptist; it was still in existence in 1125. St Aldhelm died in Doulting, near Shepton Mallet, in 709, and was buried at his request in Malmesbury. With

a nucleus of a settlement, Frome began to grow. There is a Domesday reference to a market here in 1086 - Frome was a natural meeting-place for the people of the surrounding areas. From before the Norman Conquest until the 12th century it was a royal borough.

With an abundance of sheep nearby on the Mendip hills, and Frome's proximity to water, cloth mills began to be established, and from the 17th century onwards they prospered and grew - at one time there were about two hundred mills, and it is said that seven wagons weekly were taken to London laden with cloth. The most powerful of the clothiers were the Sheppard family, who produced cloth for close on two hundred years. The increasing work force needed for spinning and weaving raised the demand for accommodation (one weaver needed between seven and eight spinners). In 1660 the

Sheppards had bought land in the old manor of St Katherine's, which enabled them to build houses and work-places. This area was, and still is, known as Sheppards Barton. Other large areas of housing were developed, notably in the Trinity area of Frome.

After the Industrial Revolution, the woollen industry was carried on in mills along the river, notably the mill at Spring Gardens, which survived until 1879. Frome was noted for its 'blue cloth', which was used for army uniforms during the Napoleonic Wars. The Russian Imperial Bodyguard were also dressed in this cloth up until the time of the Crimean War. The dye was obtained from woad, which was grown between West End and Vallis Way. Teasels were used for raising the nap of the cloth, and they grew abundantly hereabouts. Fullers earth, which was used in the washing of the wool, was obtained from Midford and Wellow.

A reluctance to modernise and remain competitive with northern manufacturers (who were willing to use new energy sources and machinery) brought about the eventual demise of Frome's woollen industry, in about 1850, after six hundred years, leaving much poverty amongst a large work force. The Poor Rate was used to sponsor emigration to Canada.

After a period of depression, Frome entered a new industrial age. Bell casting and foundry work goes back to the late 17th century, and survived for almost three hundred years. It originated from when Lewis Cockey, from Warminster, moved to Frome. Over sixty church towers in Somerset, Wiltshire and Dorset show on their bells the mark of Cockey, a foundry which later expanded into general cast iron production and also into considerable involvement in the emerging gas industry. The first gas lighting was in 1831.

The mid 19th century brought different industries to Frome, ranging from the making of brewery equipment to the production of stained glass by Horwoods in Bridge Street. J W Singer (not of sewing machine fame!) built up a fine reputation for intricate casting work, ranging from the Boadicea monument on the Thames Embankment to the ornamental screen in the Lady Chapel of St John the Baptist Parish Church in Frome. The business closed quite recently, despite diversification.

Another industry which survived the demise of the woollen industry was printing. In 1795 a local chemist, Abraham Crocker, needing stationery supplies, is thought to have obtained them from his brother Samuel, a printer. Seeing a local market for such goods, Abraham then set up a small printing business, which prospered and was later inherited by his sons John and James; James Crocker further expanded into a book business and a library. The whole undertaking was later bought by W P Penny, and survived until the turn of the century.

Another printing business began in 1845, when two business partners, Langford and Butler, started printing as a side-line to their chemist and druggist

business in Bath Street. This side-line developed into a publishing business, which produced a series of Frome Almanacks and later the Frome Sentinel. When Langford retired, Butler found a new partner, Joseph Tanner, and their joint efforts resulted in the largest printing works in the west country, Butler and Tanner. Other names such as Fussells, the edge tool manufacturers, and Wallington and Weston, who took over Houston Mills and later transferred to plastics and became members of the Marley Tile Group, have made significant contributions to Frome's economic growth.

With this industrial expansion came a need for community services such as a reliable water supply, a Public Health Department and hospital facilities, as well as energy supplies available to the general public. These arrived progressively. Gas came in 1831, followed by a fire service in 1862. The old hospital opened in Castle Street in 1875, and the Urban District Council was appointed in 1894. The century closed without electricity, however, which did not arrive until 1904.

Prominent families and significant events, catastrophes and natural phenomena all provide a plentiful supply of place names. Frome's streets, areas and monuments all pay homage to these sources, many of which are then forgotten, leaving only their names to posterity. The word 'barton' historically meant an enclosure, but within Frome's boundary it occurs frequently as a place name.

Sheppards Barton is a large area of housing adjoining Catherine Hill. Merchants Barton was the site of a silk mill: Thomson and Le Gros employed over a hundred staff, and the site later became a light industrial estate. Plumbers Barton is named after John Plomer, who lived there in 1670.

There have been many notable people in Frome, both religious and lay. St Aldhelm has already been mentioned - he brought Christianity to the area. Thomas Ken, Bishop of Bath and Wells, had sworn allegiance to James II and was unable to do so to William III. Deprived of his living, he fled to Longleat, and was protected by Lord Weymouth. The Bishop was very well regarded and retained the sympathy of the public, as we can see from the care taken to protect his grave in St John's churchyard. Later, the grave was enclosed by an iron canopy during the time of Vicar Bennett: on arriving in Frome in 1852, he was horrified at the state of St John's Church and during the next ten years virtually rebuilt it. Frome became a large non-conformist area. This was demonstrated when Dr Humfry, Minister of St John's, was unable to accept the Act of Uniformity in 1662; he left the church with other members of the congregation, which resulted in Rook Lane Congregational Chapel being built in 1707. John Wesley preached in Frome many times during the years between 1752 and 1778.

After the dissolution of the monasteries, lands owned by the church passed to the already wealthy

landowners, most notably the Thynne family of Longleat and the Horners of Mells. The Champneys of Orchardleigh were already great landowners. So were the Hungerfords, whose motto, 'time trieth troth', is now the town's motto. Other great landowners were the Earls of Cork and Orrery, who owned the Marston Estate. Lands later sold by these estates have largely decided the future development of Frome. For example, Bath Street is named after the Marquis of Bath.

A very notable figure in Frome was Thomas Bunn. He was born in 1767, a solicitor who never practised. He is mainly noted for his vision of Frome as a rival to Bath, as he greatly admired Georgian architecture. He planned a broad central avenue lined with trees leading to a great crescent, which was to be built on the ridge known as Golden Knoll. He had four ornate stone pillars built, of which only one remains today in Christchurch Street, opposite Rook House, home to the poet Elizabeth Rowe until her death in 1737. Another poet, Christina Rossetti, lived for some time in Brunswick Terrace in Fromefield, and ran a school there from April 1853 until March 1854. The first school in Frome was the free grammar school, founded in 1548.

James Wickham, a leading townsman, along with other town notables, founded the now famous Blue House. Originally an alms house, it became a charitable school for boys; their uniform was made from the famous blue cloth of Frome.

So Frome has survived through many changes, although its population has remained relatively unchanged. It can now boast more listed buildings than any other town in Somerset, despite the fact that the early 1960s saw the beginning of the Trinity clearances. These caused such a local outcry that a halt was put on the demolition. The result is that the buildings and streets that did remain have been restored and renovated, leaving us with a most important collection of 17th- and 18th-century industrial housing.

William Cobbett once referred to Frome as being 'a sort of little Manchester'. If he could ride again to this Somerset town, he would see that Frome has managed to dignify what remains of its past industrial and residential architecture, going a long way to putting it on the tourist map, the new industry for the new century.

Frome to Orchardleigh

Market Place 1907 58843
This is a quiet scene for the centre of a market
town. The present Market Place dates from 1810.
The car alongside the water trough outside the
Bull Hotel could be the Achilles, which was made
in Frome during this time. Boyle Cross in the foreground was originally a fountain erected in 1871;
the building behind it is Gilbeys Wines and Spirits.

Market Place c1950 F58005
There have been changes since 1907. Gilbey's was demolished
for road widening, and motorised transport is in evidence; road
surfaces are much improved and clearly marked. The portico to
the George Hotel was demolished after damage to it by a runaway
lorry. Telephone kiosks (now gone, sad to say) sit alongside
the Post Office, formerly the Bull Hotel.

Market Place c1950 F58003
This is a rare sight now - a baby in a pram left unattended outside a shop. Woolworths store, on the left, opened in 1934, and remains to this day. The tall chimney in the background is the old electricity works, now demolished. Narrow Stony Street lies between the National and Provincial Bank and the Pearl Assurance House building. In the distance Bath Street curves away to the left.

Market Place c1965
F58059
A market has been held in Frome since 1086. The ice-cream van amid the stalls is probably Paniccias, in Frome since 1926. A friendly policeman waves children across the road. The old George sign has now been replaced by one displaying St George and the Dragon.

Bath Street 1907
58844
This street was
named after the
Marquis of Bath, whose
coat-of-arms can be
seen above Morris
the ironmongers. Bath
Street was modelled
on nearby Bath, and
it is indeed very
elegant with its
Georgian facades.
The original Post Office
on the right was later
moved to the Market
Place. The horse and
trap and the early
automobile sit happily
alongside each other.

Bath Street 1949

F58022

There have been some changes in the 40 years since No 58844. Clothing is very different, especially for women. The Southern Electricity Service and Frome Selwood Permanent Building Society were very important to the people of Frome at that time. The sports shop window further down is attracting great interest. Devon House on the left was still a butchers shop until very recently.

Bath Street 1907 58845
The 17th-century cottages are all that remain of an area which was originally a muddy warren of lanes and alleys, which was to become Bath Street. The area was undercut after the Turnpike Act of Parliament in 1810 to provide a better road system. The cedar was planted by Thomas Bunn in 1814. In the distance is Rook Chapel.

Bath Street c1955 F58043
Note how little change there has been since photograph 58845, which was taken around 48 years before.

Rook Lane Chapel c1960 F58052
This rather grand, non-conformist chapel was built in 1707 by
the members of St John's Church who were unable to accept the
Uniformity Act. The chapel has recently been restored after having
fallen into a bad state of repair. The Public Baths (right) were built
on the old Cockey Foundry site; they opened in 1899, one of the
first swimming baths in the country.

◄ **St John's Church 1907**
58854
The stone screen, designed by Sir Jeffrey Wyatville in Tudor Gothic style, was built in 1814 to dignify the entrance to St John's. There has been a church on this site for 1300 years. The present one dates from 1100, but was largely rebuilt 100 years ago. The iron gates and railings were later removed to fuel the war effort.

Bath Street c1960 F58044
Looking down the street past the 17th-century cottages, we can clearly see the stone screen to St John's Church. The cedar tree is beginning to overshadow the far cottages, and the electricity works chimney dominates the skyline.

St John's Church the Screen 1907 ▶
58857
The rood screen, erected in 1892, was made by craftsmen in Oberammergau. It is a good example of Victorian high church restoration. It replaced a beautiful corona made by John W Singer, which was hung under the chancel arch.

St John's Church the Lady Chapel 1907
58858
This is the oldest part of the church; it was rebuilt in the 19th century in the Gothic style after having fallen into a state of disrepair. The statue of the Madonna and Child is now under the stained glass window on the left; it has been replaced by a reredos, which was given by a generous benefactress in 1924.

▼ **Gentle Street c1960** F58053

This historic route into Frome, originally called Hunger Lane, meaning 'land on a steep slope', later took its name from the Gentell family. The house with the fine Venetian windows is Argyll House (1766); next is Oriel Lodge (1800). Further up the slope, the London stage coach used to leave from the Wagon and Horses, a 16th-century inn.

▼ **Bath Street c1960** F58047

The house at the end of the 17th-century cottages gives onto Rook Lane. It is now almost hidden from view behind tall hedging and trees with a very secret garden. Behind the cottages are the Victoria Baths, opened in 1899.

▲ **Bath Street c1965**
F58065
The building advertising 'restaurant' and 'confectionery' which spans the corner into Palmer Street was the old Co-operative. It included many shops - a butcher's, a grocer's, a milliner's, a shoe shop and a furniture shop. The building now awaits restoration. On the right, Richards Menswear displays a modern shop blind.

◀ **Bath Street c1949** F58023
Look closely at this view.
We can see that the camera
is now nearer to the two
women than in F58022
(pages 24-25) - the lady
in front was originally
obscured by them. The
couple outside the sports
shop are still talking.
Fear Hills, drapers from
Trowbridge who have been
here since the 1920s, can
be seen bottom left next to
Cork Street.

◀ **Quaint Stone Houses c1950** F58011
These late 19th-century houses were in Broad Street, and were demolished during the Trinity clearances in the early 1960s. The stone portico in the far distance is the entrance to the school in Milk Street. We may be thankful that not all houses were lost to the clearances; those that remain have been sympathetically modernised.

Cork Street c1955 F58042
This street was named in honour of the 8th Earl of Cork and Orrery. The Gaumont Cinema and the Tool and Gauge Centre were demolished when the Westway shopping centre was built in 1974. Ahead is Singers (now empty), whose decorative metal works include the renowned Boadicea group on the Thames embankment. The road ahead leads to what was the St Louis Convent.

Welshmill Bridge 1907 58860
Welshmill was probably named after Welsh migrants. This serene view belies the fact that this was a busy industrial area until 1914, accommodating cloth mills, dye houses, a foundry and gas works.

St Mary the Virgin Church 1907 58859
From Welshmill, going up Innox Hill, you discover this lovely church built in 1864 and designed in early English style by the Frome-born architect C E Giles. Sad to say, the trees have been felled.

◄ **Spring Gardens 1907**
58861
This is Cape Farm, established as a ten-acre holding in 1770 and rebuilt in 1987. The man leaning on the door post may be posing for this photograph. The house on the left remains much the same today. The former Dolphin Inn further down was frequently damaged by flooding from the River Frome.

From Innox Hill 1907
58840
The foreground of this view is now entirely obscured by trees and hedging. The railway line is no longer visible. The spire in the middle background is the church of St John the Baptist. The chimneys to the right of the area are a reminder of Frome's industrial past.

▼ Spring Gardens 1907
58863
Peaceful now, this view shows the remains of the once-busy Shepherds Mill which lay on land between the Mells and the Frome Rivers. The mill closed in 1879, and the stone was later used for house building in Frome.

◄ Spring Gardens 1907
58862
This is the third of four bridges in this area. The furthermost crosses a ruined leat, a channel carrying water to a nearby mill. The river in the foreground is the Mells, and the girl in working clothes on the bridge was possibly employed at the nearby brush factory, previously Jeffries Woollen Mill.

Orchardleigh House c1965 F58078
The Champneys family owned the Orchardleigh estate from 1440 until 1839. The present house, two and a half miles north of Frome, was built by William Duckworth in 1856. The house has a French chateau appearance from this angle. Today its future remains undecided.

Orchardleigh Park c1965 F58075
The last of the Champneys family, Sir Thomas Mostyn, made many alterations to the park including the creation of the lake and a moat around the church. Sir Henry Newbolt the poet, author of the patriotic and stirring 'Drake's Drum', is buried in the churchyard. A large area of the park is now a golf course.

Rode to Longleat

Rode
The Village c1960 R406012
The village lies to the north-west, behind St Lawrence's Church.
According to local legend, Charles Stuart came through the
village after his defeat at the battle of Worcester and viewed the
surrounding countryside from the 15th-century embattled tower
of the church. Rode, which lies in the valley of the Frome, was
formerly busy in the cloth industry.

▼ Hemington, The Church c1960 H509015

The hamlet of Hemington is home to the parish church of St Mary. The parish includes the manors of Highchurch, Huntminster and Faulkland. The church was originally built by the Normans, and underwent considerable extension and alteration between 1230 and 1500 when the tower was built. The porch is a Victorian addition.

▼ Beckington, Main Street c1950 B402007

The bus is travelling the road to Bath. Much of the peacefulness of this photograph has returned since the opening of the new by-pass. The garage and forecourt still remain. New houses replace the house in the left foreground. The house across the road has a mansard roof, which would have allowed a loom to operate in the upper storey.

▲ Beckington, Frome Road c1950 B402009

This village, originally known as a town, has many fine stone houses; like its neighbour Frome, which lies 3 miles away, it was a thriving wool town, said at one time to have had five working factories. The store on the right, although unchanged, is today a private house.

**Beckington
Ravenscroft School
c1950** B402004
This handsome mansion
house, known as
Beckington Castle, dates
from the 16th century.
Probably built by a wealthy
clothier, the building is
three-storied with gabled
attics and medieval-style
battlements above the
porch and stair turrets.
Ravenscroft, a boys'
preparatory school, was
there for many years.

Beckington
Church Hill c1950 B402002
This pretty row of weavers' cottages remains unchanged today. The
building in the far distance is the Old Church House. The medieval
church of St George, a fine building with a rare Norman tower, lies
to the right behind the trees. Samuel Daniel, the Elizabethan poet,
is buried in Beckington.

Beckington, The Village c1950 B402006

Beckington, Warminster Road c1950 B402008
The Woolpack Inn, a medieval building, is situated where several roads meet. Its name suggests obvious links with past local industry, and its beers were supplied by Frome United Ales. The telephone kiosk, street light and petrol pumps are no longer there. The cottages are now all private dwellings - the one with the shop blind has a pretty bay window today.

Longleat, Shearwater Tea Gardens c1966 L190095

Longleat, Shearwater Tea Gardens c1966 L190094
Shearwater Lake, on the Longleat Estate, can be glimpsed through the trees, a popular area for sailing and walking.
The Tea Gardens are a welcome stop for an ice-cream or a pot of tea.

Horningsham, St John the Baptist Church c1955 H487081
Although there has been a church here since 1154, the early building has undergone almost total reconstruction, and only parts of the original tower remain unaltered. The newly-restored church was consecrated on 1 October 1844, and provides commanding views of the surrounding countryside. The cottage on the left is now covered with wisteria.

Horningsham, Old Cottages c1955 H487007
This row of three cottages is in Church Street. They are set slightly below road level, and are reached by steps down. The thatch remains in excellent condition, and so do the porches. The picket fence has been extended to replace the hedging. Horningsham is a beautiful village, still retaining an almost feudal air.

Longleat House c1966 L190085
Built in the 16th century on the site of an old priory from which the house gets its name, Longleat is regarded as a fine example of Elizabethan architecture. Longleat has had many distinguished visitors, including George III and his family in 1789 and Nicholas I, Tsar of Russia, in 1844.

Longleat House c1966 L190027
Here we see Longleat from afar. It sits comfortably in 900 acres of landscaped grounds, which were designed by Capability Brown. Owing to the foresight of the Sixth Marquis of Bath, Longleat was opened to the public in 1949, the first privately-owned house in England to do so on a regular basis.

Longleat
The Lions c1966 L190074
The Safari Park, one of the first of its kind in Europe, opened
in 1966. Jimmy Chipperfield of circus fame, an expert on
wildlife, was responsible for the running of the park. Tickets
at that time cost £1 per car.

Back
to Frome

Christ Church Street 1907 58847
This area was known as 'behind town' before the
building of Christ Church. The boys wearing the blue
school uniform were a familiar sight at this time,
as were the delivery carts. The tall pillar, behind the
cart, is all that survives of Thomas Bunn's vision
of a Frome that would rival Bath. Rook House on
the right was the home of Elizabeth Rowe, the poet.

Christ Church c1950 F58026
This Church was built in 1818 in the Gothic style to a design by Underwood, a little-known architect, in order to meet the religious needs of a growing population. Christ Church has been altered and enlarged, but the rather squat design of the tower remains unchanged and open to criticism.

Christ Church Street West c1955 F58035
This view shows how the street had a mixture of commerce and private residences. In the distance stands the ancient Pack Horse Inn. The ivy-clad house is now the Conservative Club, whilst the shops remain relatively unchanged. On the right is South Parade; the notice above directs us to Sheppards Barton Chapel.

Sheppards Barton c1950 F58012

The Sheppards, leading clothiers in Frome, developed this area in the 18th and 19th centuries to provide work places and living accommodation for their weavers. This road is now all paved, and the houses have been well restored. Hanging baskets and window boxes now soften the exteriors.

◄ **Catherine Hill c1950**
F58013
This street was named after St Catherine's chapel, which was dissolved in 1548. It is a busy shopping area, and many sun blinds advertising shop wares are in evidence. The sign holder to S C Roberts, Confectioner, still remains, but the gilded Hovis sign has gone. Frisbys, in the distance, continued to sell shoes until the 1970s. The hill is now pedestrianised, a delightful place to wander.

Stony Street c1950
F58014
This street is so called because it was the first paved way in Frome - originally it was a main route out. Note the Cockey lamp bracket spanning the street. The Olivers Shoes sign has gone, but Olivers continue to trade to this day in the Market Place. The notice in the window of the Star Supply Stores indicates post-war rationing. The Maypole Stores is another familiar sight.

Market Place c1965
F58080
The white building right of centre is the office of the Frome Somerset Standard, 'serving the community since 1886'. The nearer building, once three storied, was Mrs Carpenter's Drapers until 1920. It is now the HSBC Bank and marks the entrance to Cheap Street.

Cheap Street c1950 F58007
The oldest trading street in Frome is traffic-free, and still retains
its medieval character with a stream running down its centre.
The dress of the pedestrians in this photograph is very evocative
of the 1950s. Note the fine arched windows of the Ellenbray Press
at the top of the street.

Cheap Street c1965   F58066

Cheap Street c1965 F58067

Cheap Street c1965 F58069
Although this view differs in being taken facing uphill, these three views are almost certainly taken within minutes - a probability supported by the presence of the cat! (see page 55 & 56). The Flora remains a restaurant, and is now named the Settle. The Crusty Loaf wall supports a fine ornamental arched overhead street lamp produced by Cockeys, a large local engineering company, in about 1890. The bakery was originally the White Hart Inn. Today overhead floral displays are a very attractive addition to the street.

The Oldest House 1907 58851

Known locally as the 'pepper pot', Mr H R Hughes' shop, said to be the oldest in Frome, sits
at the top of Cheap Street and Eagle Lane. His wares are well advertised in both windows.
Today the stone-tiled roof retains its pepper pot shape, but a mock-Tudor upper storey and
modern windows below spoil its charm.

Via Crucis c1960 F58055
We are on the steps to St John's Church. The trees in the distance show the closeness of Frome centre to the countryside. The Via Crucis on the right looks down on the Ellenbray Press, founded by Charles Bray and named after his daughter Ellen. The fine arched windows afford excellent views of his merchandise to passers by.

◄ **St John's Church, North Side 1907** 58853
Steps lead up to the north porch of St John's Church. The Via Crucis is an unusual feature in an English churchyard. Designed and sculpted by Forsyth, and erected in 1866, it depicts six episodes of Christ's road to Calvary. The neat churchyard above the Via Crucis is now rather overgrown with trees.

Cheap Street 1907 58850 ►
We are looking back down Cheap Street. Vincents the fishmonger is now the Settle bakery - notice the stall-like appearance of the shop. The Albion Inn, one of two inns in the street, is now the Settle restaurant. Opposite, with a jettied timber-framed upper storey supported by brackets, is one of the oldest buildings in Frome, now Amicas gift shop.

◀ **Market Place 1952** F58032
We are looking towards the
bridge. To the right of it lies
the Blue House, with North
Parade in the distance. Before
the river was re-aligned,
flooding was a problem; water
used to come up as far as the
Crown Inn (centre left). The
future Edward VII put up here
in 1858. Boots the Chemist
have moved to replace Dates
the ironmongers.

◀ **The Blue House 1949** F58021
This is a splendid picture of the
Blue House, architecturally one
of the most important buildings
in Frome, dating from 1728. It
occupies the site of a previous
alms house founded in 1461 by
William Leversedge. The north
and south wings housed poor
women, whilst the central area
was a charitable boarding school,
later becoming fee-paying. The
uniform for the women and
boys was made from the famous
blue cloth of Frome. The school
closed in 1921.

▼ **The Bridge 1957** F58041
There has been a bridge
here over the River Frome
since the Middle Ages.
An unusual aspect of the
bridge are the three-storey
houses, dating from the
19th century. The road
opposite leads to Willow
Vale. The bunting probably
means that it is carnival
time, which is held annually
in September; the first
carnival was held in 1927.

◀ **Willow Vale 1907**
58849
This quiet scene belies
the fact that behind the
camera Willow Vale gives
way to the busy town
mill. The boarded-up
shop is now a thriving
cycle shop. The stone
bridge parapet has
been replaced by blue
railings. T Walls, whose
sign advertises the livery
stables, was closely
associated with the
Misses Bull, who ran a
restaurant in the Bull
Hotel.

Willow Vale c1955 F58039

There has been no great change since photograph No 58849 was taken. The ivy has been removed from the gabled house, which at one time belonged to the livery stables. Note the lifebelt, extreme right, a necessity at this time because of flooding after heavy rain. The river was realigned in 1969. The Cockey railings remain, but the footbridges have gone.

Willow Vale c1965 F58072

Beyond the industrial area are some of the most beautiful houses in Frome, which date from about 1700. Willow Vale House still retains its ivy. The later building, on the left, is now much improved in appearance by an open fretwork balcony and sympathetically painted woodwork.

From Willow Vale 1907 58842
The mineral railway line (by the far telegraph pole), constructed
in 1854, is now a private line for a local quarry. The area on the
right has since become Frome Millenium Green, a quiet place for
contemplation amidst the wildlife, set with stones, inscribed with
poetry by Christina Rossetti and Siegfried Sassoon.

◄ **The Bridge
and Market Place c1965**
F58063
The scooter is king of the
road. The rider is glancing
towards the Blue Boar Inn,
which dates from 1691.
The International Stores are
opposite under
the elaborate striped
awning. The Curry's van
is no doubt delivering to
their store in Stony Street.
High above in Palmer Street
is Kelseys, the furniture
store. Above again is Christ
Church Street West.

◄ From Willow Vale
1907 58841

An idyllic rural scene from Rodden meadow on the edge of town. In the middle distance is the spire of St John's. On the left we can glimpse the River Frome. Today this view is entirely obscured by trees.

▼ Christ Church Street West c1950
F58025

This street was named after the church, which was erected in 1818 on Packhorse field. The church lies behind the trees on the left. The Packhorse Inn can be seen in the distance on the right - its customers are perhaps waiting for opening time! The sign on the left-hand building is advertising the Somerset Smithy, whose work is known far and wide. The single-storey building we can glimpse through the trees is the fire station, which moved in 1970 to Butts Hill.

◄ Vallis Way c1950
F58024

The historic Swan Inn, left of centre, was mentioned in the Frome Rate Book of 1663. The decorative lamp in the foreground on the right has now gone. Dog food and tobacco advertisements are much in evidence on the shop fronts, and we can see the Vallis Tea Rooms above the tobacconist.

Vallis Way c1955
F58038
Since 1950 the Swan boasts a new roof line and a large sign, but later in the 1960s the building was demolished. Further up are old merchants' houses, one bearing the town motto 'time trieth troth'. There has been little change to the shops.

◄ **Vallis Vale
On the River 1907**
58867
Although a large quarry operated here from 1894 until the last war, Vallis Vale was nevertheless a popular beauty spot within walking distance of Frome, and still is today. A rock face, famous for its geological unconformity, is now a site of Special Scientific Interest.

▼ **Vallis Vale Bridge 1907** 58865
We are looking downstream to below the confluence of the River Mells and Egford Brook, tributaries of the River Frome. The cradle bridge has been replaced by a metal structure, but the stone pier remains. Downstream there was once a rifle range for the East Somerset Yeomanry.

▲ **Vallis Vale
The Waterfall 1907**
58864

◄ Vallis Vale, Cottages 1907
58866
This area known as Bedlam at the northern end of Vallis Vale belies the scene today. There was once a thriving woollen mill here, known as Riffords Mill; it was noted in 1892 to be falling into decay. All that remains today is a crumbling stone wall and traces of a sluice gate, - it is now a very peaceful place.

Mells
to Nunney

Mells, The Village 1907 58872
The pony and trap is travelling the road to Frome,
which lies three and a half miles to the east. Mells,
like its neighbour, was a hive of industry, with many
mills involved in the cloth trade. Fussell's produced
edge tools in the Wadbury Valley near Mells
until 1894. Hedging behind the stone walls now
obscures this view.

**Mells, Woodlands End
c1950** M56016
Here six roads meet.
By now the car has
replaced the pony and
trap. The road ahead
leads to the centre of
Mells. The fine houses
are an indication of
Mells's prosperity
during the time when the
woollen industry
was thriving.

Mells, The Church 1907 58874

A view of the south porch. St Andrew's Church was built in the latter part of the 15th century of oolitic limestone in the Perpendicular style. Buried in the graveyard now is Monsignor Ronald Knox, who lived for a time at the Manor. Siegfried Sassoon and Lady Violet Bonham Carter are also buried here.

Mells, From The River 1907 58873

This is a good view of the village and St Andrew's church. Note the pony and trap setting off for the road to Frome to the left of what is now a general store and post office. On the riverbank there is now a small pumping station.

Mells, The Church the Interior 1907 58875

The church was restored in the 19th century when part of the roofing was renewed. A stone pulpit replaced the earlier wooden one, and the old Jacobean pews were largely replaced with new ones. Each of the pew ends are different, and were carved in the village. The stained glass for the windows was also produced locally.

◄ **Mells, The Memorial c1950** M56020
Further up the hill from the manor is the very fine war memorial, designed by Lutyens in c1920. The central column is crowned by the figure of St George and the Dragon. Circular memorial plaques on either side on the wall commemorate both World Wars.

Mells, The Manor and the Church c1965
M56037
Mells Manor, largely Elizabethan, was built on the site of a medieval monastic manor. It was rebuilt in the 16th century by John Horner of nursery rhyme fame, who acquired three manors at the time of the Dissolution of the Monasteries. Burne-Jones (1833-1898), a frequent visitor to the manor, is said to have painted a piano there.

Mells, Gay Street c1950 M56019
This gabled thatched cottage is very typical of the area. Thatch was used before tile and slate. This cottage might be a local store, as the bottom sign is advertising Typhoo Tea. The street remains much the same today.

Mells, Little Green c1950 M56013
These cottages lie on the road down from the school, one of the first church schools in Somerset. The thatch looks so picturesque today. The signpost beyond directs the driver to Frome on the right and Coleford to the left. The 'halt' sign looks less strident than those we are used to today.

▼ Mells, Little Green c1965 M56039

Turn left by the car in picture M56013, and you pass this pretty row of cottages, probably built of the local oolitic limestone, as most buildings here are. The house on the left is the old forge, and the tree between it and its neighbour has been removed; so has the cottage with the derelict thatch.

▼ Holcombe, Brewery Road c1950 H92006

Coming from Mells, one enters Holcombe via Brewery Road, which takes its name from the well-known Holcombe Brewery started by Mr J A Green in 1800 to supply local workmen from the mines and quarries. The first house on the left stands today behind high hedging. Note the wattle fencing so popular today.

▲ Holcombe, The School c1955 H92012

The Methodist Church lies behind the school building, a reminder of the non-conformity in this area. Holcombe's name is derived from the Anglo-Saxon for 'hollow, or deep, combe': the village originally lay one and a half miles lower down, but the plague forced the survivors to re-site the village to its present position. A local pub is called the Ring of Roses; the name comes from the nursery rhyme, which describes the fate of the plague victims.

Holcombe, The Hill c1950
H92004

The road leads on through Holcombe Village and down the steep valley side to Edford Green. Following a vehicle accident, the Post Office now has a large plate glass window which replaced the one we see here. The wall still retains the letter box and the Parish Council notice board. Further up the hill lies Holcombe Manor, which was home to the family of Scott of the Antarctic. His parents are buried in the graveyard of the old church of St Andrew, which lies on the site of the original village.

**Stoke St Michael
The Square and Stoke
Hill c1950** S789007
As we come down
into the centre of the
village, we see the
Knatchbull Arms on the
right, a 17th-century
inn with stone mullion
windows and gabled
dormers. The then
modern shop, right of
centre, is now a general
store and Post Office.
The telephone box,
which does mar the
front of the inn, has
been removed.

Stoke St Michael
Stoke Hill c1950 S789002
Situated on the Mendip Hills, the village was originally called Stoke Lane, and has always been surrounded by quarries. The fields in the distance are where photograph S789015, (page 83) was taken from. The cottages remain little changed today with pretty gardens above the stone walls. The standpipe, no longer needed, has gone.

Stoke St Michael
The Knatchbull Arms and Church Street c1950
S789004
There are advertisements and the Parish Council notice board on the wall of the inn. The church, in the distance, gives its name to the village. A Norman building originally, it was replaced by one in the Early English style. On the right, behind the stone wall, there is now a small memorial garden with a stream running through its centre.

Stoke St Michael
The Square c1950
S789006
Of these three shops, only the one on the right remains today, a butcher's shop. At one time there were three bakers in the village, and bread was delivered by horse and trap. We have a good view of the inn sign, the coat-of-arms of the Knatchbull family, which depicts two pigs climbing up an apple tree.

◄ **Nunney, The Village and the Castle 1907**
58877
Nunney, lying just south-west of Frome, has a fine medieval church and the romantic ruins of a castle. The George Inn sign spans the entire road, clearly indicating its position. During the prosperity of the wool trade in Frome, work was farmed out to people in Nunney; clothiers called weekly delivering wool and collecting spun yarn.

◀ **Stoke St Michael General View c1950** S789015
This photograph was taken from the road to Leigh-on-Mendip, originally home to the Knatchbull family. We can see Stoke Lane in the distance. In the past this area has seen saw yards, tan yards, a paper mill and an edge tool mill. A local corn mill was powered by the village stream. The field in the foreground has recently been planted with trees.

▲ **Nunney, From the Bridge 1907** 58879
The church lies behind a huddle of dilapidated cottages lining the Nunney Brook; here, wool was washed during the busy years of the cloth trade. Today the cottages are all restored. They have small gardens overlooking the brook, which is home to many ducks.

◀ **Nunney, The Castle c1960** N52015
The castle, surrounded by a moat, was fortified and crenellated in the French Bastille style by Sir John de la Mare in 1373. It was a Royalist stronghold during the Civil War; it was attacked by the Roundheads and then 'slighted' (rendered unusable). The most attractive manor house on the left dates from the 18th century, but it is thought to have medieval origins.

◄ **Nunney**
The Village c1955 N52007
In the centre stands the bridge spanning Nunney Brook. The top of Horn Street is in the middle distance, and on the bend is the entrance to Rockfield House. On the extreme right is the Wesley Chapel, dating from 1812, now a workshop. The last house top left, the Vicarage, is now a residential home for the elderly.

Nunney, The Village and the Castle 1907 58876

A good view of the ivy-covered castle, showing its ruined state. The present All Saints Church originates from between the 13th and 15th centuries, although a fragment of a Saxon cross may pre-date the site to before the Norman Conquest. The field in the foreground has been lost to housing.

Nunney, Market Place c1955 N52008

In 1260 a licence was granted for a market to be held weekly in Nunney. The thatched cottage, known as Beehive House, was originally a turnpike house. There is a water tap in the archway below the signpost. The ladies carrying flowers are probably attending a funeral; coffins at this time were carried by pall bearers to the church.

Nunney, Bell House and the Castle c1960 N52020

This view was taken from the bottom of Horn Street. On the left is Bell House, medieval in origin. Opposite Bell House, and out of the picture, is the guard house, a small lock-up built in 1824. This view of the castle shows how low-lying it is, not in a good defensible position.

Nunney, The Brook and the Bridge c1955 N52003
The brook, this side of the three-arched bridge, looks to be in flood compared with picture 58879 (page 83). The cottage on the left is one of a row fronting onto Horn Street. Beehive House retains its thatch to the present day. The building on the right is now the village grocery store.

Nunney, Frome Road from the Church Tower c1960 N52016
Here we see Nunney at the north-east end. The house in the foreground, built in 1820, was the church school house until 1896, when it became known as the Church Rooms. The lane on the left is locally called Donkey Lane; it leads to one of the mill sites belonging to the Fussells Ironworks. The road out takes you back to Frome.

Index

FROME

Bath Street 22-23, 24-25, 26, 27, 28-29, 30-31

Blue House 62

Bridge 63, 66

Broad Street 32

Catherine Hill 49

Cheap Street 54, 55, 56, 57, 58, 59, 61

Christ Church 48

Christ Church Street 46-47, 48, 67

Cork Street 32-33

Gentle Street 30

Innox Hill 34-35

Market Place 6-17, 18, 19, 20-21, 30, 52-53, 62-63, 66

Orchardleigh House 36

Rook Lane Chapel 26, 27

St John's Church 28, 29, 60

St Mary the Virgin Church 33

Sheppards Barton 49

Spring Gardens 34, 35

Stony Street 50-51

Vallis Vale 70-71

Vallis Way 67, 68-69

Via Crucis 60

Welshmill Bridge 32

Willow Vale 63, 64, 65, 66-67

AROUND FROME

Beckington 38-39, 40, 41

Hemington 38

Holcombe 78-79

Horningsham 43

Longleat 42, 44, 45

Mells 72-73, 74-75, 76-77, 78

Nunney 82, 83, 84-85, 86

Rode 37

Stoke St Michael 80-81, 82-83

FRITH PRODUCTS & SERVICES

Francis Frith would doubtless be pleased to know that the pioneering publishing venture he started in 1860 still continues today. Over a hundred and forty years later, The Francis Frith Collection continues in the same innovative tradition and is now one of the foremost publishers of vintage photographs in the world. Some of the current activities include:

INTERIOR DECORATION

Today Frith's photographs can be seen framed and as giant wall murals in thousands of pubs, restaurants, hotels, banks, retail stores and other public buildings throughout the country. In every case they enhance the unique local atmosphere of the places they depict and provide reminders of gentler days in an increasingly busy and frenetic world.

PRODUCT PROMOTIONS

Frith products are used by many major companies to promote the sales of their own products or to reinforce their own history and heritage. Frith promotions have been used by Hovis bread, Courage beers, Scots Porage Oats, Colman's mustard, Cadbury's foods, Mellow Birds coffee, Dunhill pipe tobacco, Guinness, and Bulmer's Cider.

GENEALOGY AND FAMILY HISTORY

As the interest in family history and roots grows world-wide, more and more people are turning to Frith's photographs of Great Britain for images of the towns, villages and streets where their ancestors lived; and, of course, photographs of the churches and chapels where their ancestors were christened, married and buried are an essential part of every genealogy tree and family album.

FRITH PRODUCTS

All Frith photographs are available Framed or just as Mounted Prints and Posters (size 23 x 16 inches). These may be ordered from the address below. Other products available are - Address Books, Calendars, Jigsaws, Canvas Prints, Postcards and local and prestige books.

THE INTERNET

Already ninety thousand Frith photographs can be viewed and purchased on the internet through the Frith websites and a myriad of partner sites.

For more detailed information on Frith products, look at this site:
www.francisfrith.com

See the complete list of Frith Books at: www.francisfrith.com
This web site is regularly updated with the latest list of publications from The Francis Frith Collection. If you wish to buy books relating to another part of the country that your local bookshop does not stock, you may purchase on-line.

For further information, trade, or author enquiries please contact us at the address below:
The Francis Frith Collection, Unit 6, Oakley Business Park, Wylye Road, Dinton, Wiltshire SP3 5EU.
Tel: +44 (0)1722 716 376 Fax: +44 (0)1722 716 881 Email: sales@francisfrith.co.uk

---

See Frith products on the internet at www.francisfrith.com

FREE PRINT OF YOUR CHOICE

Mounted Print
Overall size 14 x 11 inches (355 x 280mm)

Choose any Frith photograph in this book.
Simply complete the Voucher opposite and return it with your remittance for £3.50 (to cover postage and handling) and we will print the photograph of your choice in SEPIA (size 11 x 8 inches) and supply it in a cream mount with a burgundy rule line (overall size 14 x 11 inches).
Please note: aerial photographs and photographs with a reference number starting with a "Z" are not Frith photographs and cannot be supplied under this offer. Offer valid for delivery to one UK address only.

PLUS: Order additional Mounted Prints at HALF PRICE - £9.50 each (normally £19.00)
If you would like to order more Frith prints from this book, possibly as gifts for friends and family, you can buy them at half price (with no additional postage and handling costs).

PLUS: Have your Mounted Prints framed
For an extra £18.00 per print you can have your mounted print(s) framed in an elegant polished wood and gilt moulding, overall size 16 x 13 inches (no additional postage and handling required).

IMPORTANT!

These special prices are only available if you use this form to order. You must use the ORIGINAL VOUCHER on this page (no copies permitted). We can only despatch to one UK address. This offer cannot be combined with any other offer.

Send completed Voucher form to:
The Francis Frith Collection, Unit 6, Oakley Business Park, Wylye Road, Dinton, Wiltshire SP3 5EU

CHOOSE A PHOTOGRAPH FROM THIS BOOK

Voucher for **FREE** and Reduced Price Frith Prints

Please do not photocopy this voucher. Only the original is valid, so please fill it in, cut it out and return it to us with your order.

Picture ref no	Page no	Qty	Mounted @ £9.50	Framed + £18.00	Total Cost £
		1	Free of charge*	£	£
			£9.50	£	£
			£9.50	£	£
			£9.50	£	£
			£9.50	£	£
			£9.50	£	£

Please allow 28 days for delivery.
Offer available to one UK address only

* Post & handling		£3.50
Total Order Cost	£	

Title of this book . . . .

I enclose a cheque/postal order for £ . . . . made payable to 'The Francis Frith Collection'

OR please debit my Mastercard / Visa / Maestro card, details below

Card Number:

Issue No (Maestro only):   Valid from (Maestro):

Card Security Number: Expires:

Signature:

Name Mr/Mrs/Ms . . . .

Address . . . .

. . . .

. . . .

. . . . Postcode . . . .

Daytime Tel No . . . .

Email . . . .

Valid to 31/12/12

Can you help us with information about any of the Frith photographs in this book?

We are gradually compiling an historical record for each of the photographs in the Frith archive. It is always fascinating to find out the names of the people shown in the pictures, as well as insights into the shops, buildings and other features depicted.

If you recognize anyone in the photographs in this book, or if you have information not already included in the author's caption, do let us know. We would love to hear from you, and will try to publish it in future books or articles.

An Invitation from The Francis Frith Collection to Share Your Memories

The 'Share Your Memories' feature of our website allows members of the public to add personal memories relating to the places featured in our photographs, or comment on others already added. Seeing a place from your past can rekindle forgotten or long held memories. Why not visit the website, find photographs of places you know well and add YOUR story for others to read and enjoy? We would love to hear from you!

www.francisfrith.com/memories

Our production team

Frith books are produced by a small dedicated team at offices near Salisbury. Most have worked with the Frith Collection for many years. All have in common one quality: they have a passion for the Frith Collection.

Frith Books and Gifts

We have a wide range of books and gifts available on our website utilising our photographic archive, many of which can be individually personalised.

www.francisfrith.com